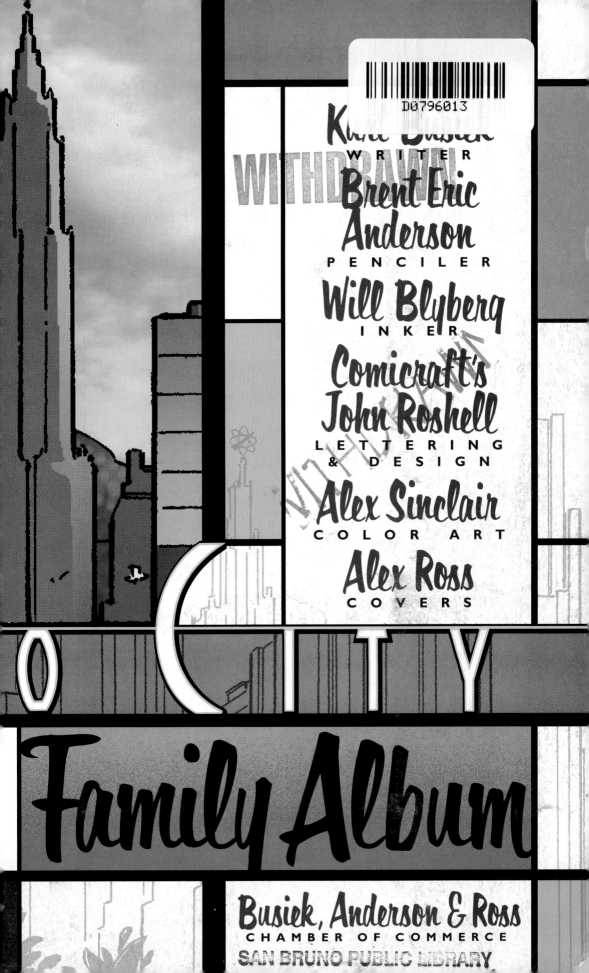

Kurt Busiek
WRITER

Brent Eric Anderson
PENCILER

Will Blyberg
INKER

Comicraft's
John Roshell
LETTERING
& DESIGN

Alex Sinclair
COLOR ART

Alex Ross
COVERS

WITHDRAWAL

O CITY

family Album

Busiek, Anderson & Ross
CHAMBER OF COMMERCE
SAN BRUNO PUBLIC LIBRARY

D0796013

Juke Box Productions

Ann Huntington Busiek
MANAGING EDITOR

Comicraft

Richard Starkings
ART DIRECTOR

Homage DC Comics

JENETTE KAHN
PRESIDENT & EDITOR-IN-CHIEF

PAUL LEVITZ
EXECUTIVE VICE PRESIDENT & PUBLISHER

JIM LEE
EDITORIAL DIRECTOR — WILDSTORM

JOHN NEE
VP & GENERAL MANAGER — WILDSTORM

SCOTT DUNBIER
GROUP EDITOR

JONATHAN PETERSON
ORIGINAL SERIES EDITOR

JOHN LAYMAN
COLLECTED EDITION EDITOR

RICHARD BRUNING
VP — CREATIVE DIRECTOR

PATRICK CALDON
VP — FINANCE & OPERATIONS

DOROTHY CROUCH
VP — LICENSED PUBLISHING

TERRI CUNNINGHAM
VP — MANAGING EDITOR

JOEL EHRLICH
SENIOR VP — ADVERTISING & PROMOTIONS

ALISON GILL
EXECUTIVE DIRECTOR - MANUFACTURING

LILLIAN LASERSON
VP & GENERAL COUNSEL

BOB WAYNE
VP - DIRECT SALES

KURT BUSIEK'S ASTRO CITY FAMILY ALBUM. THIRD PRINTING. ISBN# 1-56389-552-8. Published by Homage Comics, an imprint of DC Comics. Editorial offices 7910 Ivanhoe, Suite 438, La Jolla, CA 92037. © 1998 Juke Box Productions, all rights reserved. Originally published as KURT BUSIEK'S ASTRO CITY volume 2 #1-3 and #10-13. KURT BUSIEK'S ASTRO CITY, its logos, symbols, prominent characters featured in this volume and the distinctive likenesses thereof, are trademarks of Juke Box Productions. Homage Comics is ™ DC Comics. Introduction copyright © 1998 by The Kilimanjaro Corporation. Any similarities to institutions or persons living or dead is unintentional and purely coincidental. PRINTED IN CANADA.
DC Comics. A division of Warner Bros. - A Time Warner Entertainment Company

Dedications

To my sisters — Amy, Robin, Faith and Jennifer — who gave me a thorough grounding in family life, and to Sydney Ann, my impending daughter, who'll teach me all about it from a new perspective.

— KURT

To Sydney, Liberty, and Stone, the newest members of the Astro City family; and to Grace and Blythe Sinclair, our most colorful additions.

— BRENT

I'm so very alone.

— ALEX

Contents

Introduction

The Roses of Heliogabalus
Sir Lawrence Alma-Tadema

by Harlan Ellison

THERE WAS A SUNNY TIME, SOME YEARS AGO, when I spent whole seasons in Astro. Some PR flack out of New York had been hired to "promote" the City, and the still, silent eye of his brainstorm campaign was to drop the "City" and just refer to it as "Astro" or, even more preposterous, "the Big A."

Fortunately, its vogue was short-lived, narrow, and went nowhere reifying. And pretty soon they fired his agency, and the billboards were gone, and the cardboard stand-ups turned yellow in barbershop windows, and those with good sense dropped it; and now, the only people who call it "the Big A" are the same species of parvenus and arrivistes who call San Francisco "Frisco" or pronounce Oregon "*ore-uh-gawn*." But some of us still fall back on calling it Astro…when no one's looking.

Don't get over to Astro City much these days. Not since I had the quadruple bypass. Can't stand travel much—and it *is* something like twelve hundred miles from L.A.—and so I've had to postpone over and over again what used to be a fairly regular hegira: to Astro City, to hang out with Kurt and Alex and, especially, Brent, who only gets goofier with age.

But there were times when we sat, all four of us, looking out on the Raboy Esplanade, in that elegant lobby cafe (the name of which I cannot, for the life of me, remember) in the big glass-and-steel office building across from the Museum, staring at the sweep and swirl of the Deco facade, talking shop, talking art, talking superfolk and dreams, talking about all the things that pass out of one's mind half an hour beyond the brilliance of camaraderie.

Oftentimes I reminisce and am lured to the conclusion that it was the presence of the Finlay-Cartier Museum of Fine Arts that inspired us so. I can't remember similar sessions of chat with other friends, in other venues, being nearly as scintillant or filled with cheer. And so, I *miss* Astro.

Good times there, good people—even if Busiek was always *kvetching* about some deadline or other—as well as something constantly happening. And the thing that *always* amazed me was that never did I—or anyone else I talked to—feel inferior to the "powered people," what citizens of Astro called "the costumes." Oh, we'd see them all the time, here and there…but mostly over there, doing their super-business, and we were over here…doing our non-super business. But it was always sort of *never the twain shall meet.*

I'll get back to all that in a minute.

Indulge me. I want to explain why it is, for me, that Astro is a very special place, a *nidus* if you will. With an explanation, by way of metaphor.

Indulge me. It's my way. I do, after all, make my not inconsiderable living by telling stories, imparting lies, cobbling up scenarios.

AFTER A BIT, SIR LAWRENCE ALMA-TADEMA, AND THAT PAINTING on loan from some private collection in the U.K. or the Netherlands, as it hung before us, the four of us, in the West Gallery of the Finlay-Cartier, many years ago. In a moment. But first. By metaphor…

In the opening decade of the twentieth century, Gustav Stickley's *The Craftsman*, a magazine that promoted lively discussion of the arts and crafts tradition in the United States, ran a series of essays by Irene Sargent, a woman of powerful critical voice, championing the design jewelry of the incomparable René Lalique. This was prior to his glass of high art we honor today.

She referred to Lalique, early on, as a "model of ingenuity, imagination, and craftsmanship." Kurt Busiek. Brent Anderson. Alex Ross. (And, one presumes, though I don't know him, Will Blyberg. Whose inclusion in all that has gone before, and all that follows, goes without saying. Because the core cadre admits no one even an iota less ingenious, imaginative, and craftwise than itself.) She said, of Lalique, that he was the avatar of "art nouveau" (a term then applied to only the most innovative in art), whose concepts "actively challenge others to surpass his achievements by setting a creative standard on a very high plateau." Kurt Busiek. Brent Anderson, goofier by the year. Alex and Will. And finally, by metaphor, this: "Taken thus for all in all, M. Lalique is an artist of that type—the creative— which appears most rarely in the course of time. He has given a new direction to the art which he practices, and indicates to those that shall succeed him alluring possibilities of beauty. He has raised the objects which he creates from the rank of toy and talismans up to that of true works of art." The cadre.

What they have done with Astro City has already become the standard to be emulated. Would that the parvenus and arrivistes had even a distant whisper of their abilities.

Imitation may well be the sincerest form of flattery, but it is also the canker on the rose. First comes the voice, then—fainter, smudged and off-key—the echo.

They have elevated toys and talismans to the very high plateau of original art. And I knew them—all but Will—when.

W E STOOD IN A LINE, THE FOUR OF US, there in the West Gallery of the Finlay-Cartier Museum on the Raboy Esplanade, and we stared at a painting on loan from some private collection in the U.K. Or the Netherlands.

It was Sir Lawrence Alma-Tadema's *The Roses of Heliogabalus.*

"Geezus!" Kurt said, softly, all breath and no syllables. "It's as if you're there. It's real. That's all it is... it's palpable."

Let me tell you about that painting. This, from the 1996 comprehensive survey of Alma-Tadema's *oeuvre*, published by the Van Gogh Museum in Amsterdam:

"Marcus Aurelius Antonius became Emperor of Rome at the age of fourteen: his more familiar name, Heliogabalus or Elagabalus, was derived from the Syrian sun god whose worship, along with Eastern court practices, he attempted to introduce to Rome. He was a voluptuary in the style of Nero and ruled Rome amidst venality and debauchery until he was murdered by the Praetorian guard after a reign of only four years (218-222 C.E.)."

Gibbon said Heliogabalus, during his brief reign,

was "alike odious and contemptible by all manner of follies and abominations." And Walter Pater called him "an embodiment of pure and unmodified evil."

Brent had the catalogue *raisonné* and, as we stood there in front of the tableau, he read to us:

"Alma-Tadema's young Emperor, dressed in saffron silk, reclines on a couch placed on a raised platform and gazes impassively at the scene below…The guests, lazily reclining on silk cushions, in an arena of pain and pleasure calmly succumb to a sea of petals and their exquisitely decadent deaths."

There was then, as there is now, such a sense of *presence* in that most chilling example of what has come to be known as the Orientalist School of painting, that I cannot express with sufficient vigor how profoundly we four were affected by that viewing, on that afternoon, so long ago.

But both Kurt and Brent—echoed by Alex—said that one day, if the opportunity presented itself, they would strive, undertake, struggle toward…a project that captured *just that* sense of time and place. A project that would encapsulate a superimposed pre-continuum, a fully-formed world.

Astro City.

C HECK OUT ONE OF THE EARLIEST SCENES in this volume. I don't know on which page the panel will fall, but it's the page on which Helia and Thunderhead leave the City and the weather clears. It's the bottom of the three panels. Take a look. That's Central Park West beyond the treetops of Central Park in Manhattan. I used to have dinner with Tony Randall in one of those buildings, and Isaac and Janet Asimov looked out of yet another, next door, directly down on The Tavern on the Green. It's New York, that panel. In Astro?

There is a street in Astro City that looks

NOW SH
THE MONS
THE DARK C
PLUS NEWSREE
SHORTS & AIR A
THE MONSTER FROM THE DARK CO

something like this view of Central Park West. Not exactly, but close. Brent has filched, what we call in the comics biz "a swipe," and he has plugged it in, because the street he *wanted* to use, the street that *used* to exist in Astro, is now gone, razed to build the elaborate International Merchandise Towers, now the hub of the City's burgeoning clothing industry. So Brent has filched, and we have a simulacrum of the way that corner of Astro City looked oh, fifteen, twenty years ago. Just around the time the four of us studied Heliogabalus's horror show. But, ironically, it is precisely *because* Brent has been compelled to use swipes that I was asked to write the introduction to this most excellent volume of work that exists on a very high plateau.

Turn, if you will, to the fourth page of the Loony Leo story (and, again, I apologize for not being able to direct you by page number). The bottom tier. You see that lovely Brent Anderson rendering of the Ace Theater on Daigh Street? Well, it's New York, again.

But this shot is inordinately special to me.

And it is the impetus for Kurt asking me to preface these fine Astro City stories.

Because I worked directly across the street from the original scene that was snapped as a photo, that Brent swiped to approximate Daigh Street back in the 1950s. (To be exact, in the photo, it's about 1939, and the film playing at the movie house Brent has recast as the Ace was *King Kong*.)

But there was virtually no change on that street between 1939 and 1954 when I worked at the Broadway Book Shop, between the Victoria and Astor Theaters, between 45th and 46th Streets, on Broadway. It's *Broadway*, folks…it's Times Square…and I hadn't yet sold my first story, I had been thrown out of Ohio State University and had come to New York to make my fortune…and I was working the most fascinating hours anyone

could work in that town…seven p.m. till two in the morning. And what a time in my life that was!

I was very poor, I was living in a one-room flat 'way uptown at 611 West 114th Street, off Broadway, across from Columbia University; and every day I would take the IRT subway down to Times Square. First, I'd stop off at the Clam Bar and Flea Circus on 42nd, and say hi to Tiny Tim— yes, the singer who became ultra-famous later with *Tiptoe Through the Tulips* and got married on the Johnny Carson show—but his name wasn't Tiny Tim in those days—but I'm afraid I can't remember what stage-name he was using when he was at the Flea Circus, singing in the basement theater—and then I'd go across 42nd and walk about two doors uptown to the pizza joint where Caruso would give me a terrific slice for 15¢, and add a large papaya juice for another dime. And that was my dinner.

Well, to be precise, it was my *early*, pre-job snack.

Then I'd stroll on uptown to the Broadway Book Shop, and begin selling switchblade knives and the Modern Library editions to tourists and passersby and actors heading to their shows up and down Schubert Alley.

And about ten or ten-thirty, I'd dash between cars on Broadway and the parallel 7th Avenue, and I'd find myself right there in the middle of Brent's swipe, at the Buitoni Spaghetti House, where I could get a swell meal—a plate of *al dente* spaghettini, with one meatball, a chunk of French bread and butter, and an iced tea—for a buck.

Look at that dear panel in the Loony Leo saga. Is it possible that I can convey to you, merest words only, what it meant to me, as I was reading that issue of *Astro City*, and turned the page and found myself staring back through the lens of memory to a scene I hadn't seen in more than forty years? I tell you only this: I am hardly the world's most sentimental soul. No patsy, I. But as I turned that page for the first time, and I let my eyes drift toward the bottom tier, I began to cry. Not hard, not painfully, but my eyes welled, and I was whisked back four decades and more, to my fledgling days as a writer, when I was struggling not only to break into print, to *become* somebody, but to scratch out a living at thirty-five dollars a week, writing all night, sleeping only two or three hours in the early afternoon, hustling my manuscripts to editors in the late afternoon and early evening, and then going off to work my brains out just to pay for that fifteen-dollar-a-week room.

All in that moment. All in that swipe Brent used to recapture the glory of the Ace in the days when Daigh Street was lively and colorful…and not a surrogate Hard Rock Disney Trump Supermall of soulless hotels and tourist crap slop shops.

You see, times change and not all change is

progress. But Brent had to reconstruct the dreamtime of Daigh Street, as this panel reconstructed for me the memory of Times Square in 1954. He *had* to filch and fudge it, to give you the panel correctly. I know he broke his ass trying to find a comparable photo of Daigh and the Ace…but it wasn't to be. So he took a photo of New York in 1939 (unchanged in 1954) and he retouched it. But *that's* why *Astro City* is the uncommon marvel that it is, no matter how many imitators think they can coat-tail themselves into that winner's circle.

It's the touchstone that brings together my tropes of Lalique and Alma-Tadema and the very high plateau upon which *Astro City* sits.

There is a reality to Astro. It is a series of comic book journeys to a *real* place. Realer (yes, improper grammar) than Metropolis or Gotham City or the New York of *Spider-Man*. Realer, perhaps, than many of the places in which you now sit, reading this.

Brent and Kurt and Alex (and now Will, too) go to Astro with regularity. They commute to that real place—as I no longer can, save in reading their work—and they come back with true snapshots of a marvelous land as exotic as Skull Island or Oz or Ultima Thule or Atlantis. They return with stories and anecdotes of ordinary folk like you and me, and the "costumes" who are anything *but* ordinary.

And the *realness* they transcribe is as much sense of place as falling into that sensuous and awful scene in which the depraved Heliogabalus suffocates his courtiers with a *tsunami* of rose petals. As exquisitely rendered in minute detail as René Lalique created his immortal jewelry.

Astro exists.

No minuscule wonder, that.

How difficult it is, as a writer—I tell you absolutely—to create that which *seems* authentic, palpable… *real*. I've been doing it most of my life, and it never grows easier. And Kurt and Brent and Alex and Will do it every issue. They go to the City, and they return with treasures, each one as small and perfect as a Lalique.

I remember my days spent with the cadre in that city of costumes and caring, decades ago, and I dream of the past, and I revel in their presenta-tions of the present. And when Brent has to go back to my past to bring forth a view of Astro that no longer exists, well, it puts me blood and bones and mouth and marrow right in the middle of a work of creativity that exists on a very high plateau indeed.

And that is why I am here. Because I used to spend a buck for dinner at the Buitoni Spaghetti House, when I was young, and the world was filled with costumes and wonder and the awe of standing before a painting that made us all understand that…it's real…geez, it's palpable!

When someone asks you "what is Art?" well, you can hand them this book; and I do not think they will treat you less than nobly for the consideration.

HARLAN ELLISON
Madison, Wisconsin
26 September 1998

HARLAN ELLISON, during a forty-plus-year career, has written 74 books, a dozen or so motion pictures, several dozen teleplays, and more than 1700 stories, essays, articles, columns and commentaries, for which he has won more awards than any other living fantasist. He is the creator of the DREAM CORRIDOR comics from Dark Horse, and a frequent, if controversial, "talking head" on such network tv shows as POLITICALLY INCORRECT and THE LATE LATE SHOW WITH TOM SNYDER. He began reading comic books in 1939.

"Welcome to Astro City"

THE *SUN'S* OUT, AND THERE'S A *BREEZE*, AND WE DON'T BOTHER TO UNPACK, WE JUST GET *OUTSIDE*.

THERE'S SOMETHING ABOUT A *NEW CITY* -- SOMETHING *CLEAN*, THAT WASHES AWAY *GRIME* AND OLD *MEMORIES* --

I WAS *BORN* HERE, MAN. WOULDN'T LIVE ANYWHERE ELSE FOR A *MILLION BUCKS*.

I WENT TO COLLEGE HERE AT *FOX-BROOME*. AND THE MINUTE I SAW THE CITY, I KNEW IT WAS *HOME*.

I GUESS IT WAS LOVE AT *FIRST SIGHT*.

SORRY, I'M IN A *HURRY*. I DON'T HAVE TIME TO TALK.

MARCY DOERR, WITH THE *KAST-TV ROVING REPORT*. AND WHY DO YOU LIVE IN ASTRO CITY, SIR?

UH --

I ALMOST SAY, *"BECAUSE IT ISN'T BOSTON,"* BUT I CATCH MYSELF.

WELL, ACTUALLY, THIS IS OUR *FIRST DAY* HERE --

"-- I GUESS WE COULD DO SOME *SIGHTSEEING*..."

AND THAT'S *AIR ACE*. HE'S THE VERY *FIRST* SUPERHERO -- FIRST WE KNOW ABOUT, ANYWAY -- AND HE WAS FROM *RIGHT HERE*.

LOOK, DADDY, *LOOK!* THAT'S *LOONY LEO*, FROM THE CARTOONS!

Loony Leo's

FROM *OLDEN DAYS*, DADDY?

NOT *THAT* OLDEN, FAITHIE -- BUT IT *WAS* A LONG TIME AGO.

THAT'S *RIGHT* -- THAT'S HIS *RESTAURANT*. I HEARD HE WAS OUT HERE, BUT I GUESS I FORGOT.

SEE -- THAT'S THE *ASTROBANK TOWER*.

THAT *ROCKET* ON TOP'S AN *EMERGENCY BEACON* -- THEY USE IT TO CONTACT THE *HEROES*, WHEN THEY NEED 'EM.

HUH. SO *THAT'S* IT...

I WISH *MOMMY* COULD SEE THIS!

UH...*YEAH*, HONEY. MAYBE *SOMEDAY*.

DADDY, WE HAVE TO GET OFF AT THE *NEXT STOP*. THERE'S A *PLAQUE*...

THE REST OF THE DAY GOES WITHOUT ANY *TROUBLE* --

DADDY! OVER BY THE SWINGS, YOU GOTTA COME *SEE!*

THERE'S ANOTHER *STATUE!*

THE *EMERGENCY BEACON* GOES OFF, AND THE LIGHT'S JUST *SWALLOWED* BY THE CLOUDS --

-- NOT THAT IT MAKES A *DIFFERENCE* --

-- BECAUSE THE HEROES ARE ALREADY *COMING* --

-- FLYING UP AT THAT CREATURE LIKE THERE'S NOTHING THAT CAN *STOP* THEM --

-- AND I NOTICE SOMETHING I NEVER *THOUGHT* ABOUT BEFORE -- THAT HERE, SEEING THEM IN *PERSON* LIKE THIS --

-- THEY LOOK SO *SMALL* --

2

"Everyday Life"

AH, **THERE** YOU ARE, ASTRA! AFTER YOU FINISH **EXERCISING**, POP INTO THE BATH AND COME TO **BREAKFAST**, CHOP-CHOP! YOU'VE GOT THAT **TV SHOW** TODAY!

OKAY, MOM!

♪ Oh, dear, what can the matter be, when it's converted to energy... ♪

WHAT'S **THIS** STUFF?

IT'S TO HELP INCREASE YOUR **ENERGY-STORAGE** LEVELS. I ASKED YOUR GRAMPA TO MAKE IT **GRAPE-**FLAVORED. IS IT?

IT'S MORE, UM, **MANGANESE-**FLAVOR. BUT THAT'S OKAY -- I'M GETTING TO **LIKE** THAT...

HERE -- LET ME ADJUST YOUR **OUTFIT...**

MOMMM, I CAN REPROGRAM MY CLOTHES **MYSELF,** YOU KNOW!

"HER GRANDFATHER IS **DR. AUGUSTUS FURST,** ONE OF THE MOST BRILLIANT **SCIENTISTS** AND DARING **ADVENTUR-ERS** IN HISTORY.

"WITH HIS BROTHER **JULIUS,** DR. FURST TRAVELED THE WORLD IN SEARCH OF **ADVENTURE** AND **KNOWLEDGE** --

"-- BUT THE TWO OF THEM DIDN'T STAY MERELY A DUO FOR *LONG!*"

"DR. FURST WAS *MARRIED*, AND *DIVORCED*, FOUR TIMES. AND IT WAS HIS *THIRD* WIFE, NADIA, WHO CHANGED HIS LIFE THE MOST --"

"-- NADIA, WHO HE FOUND TRAPPED IN A FIELD OF *ALIEN ENERGY* IN *YUGOSLAVIA*."

"HE *RESCUED* HER, FELL IN LOVE, MARRIED HER --"

"-- AND WITHIN TWO YEARS, SHE *LEFT* HIM, FOR THE PRINCE OF A NEAR-LEGENDARY TRIBE OF *ANIMAL-MEN.*"

"BUT THE STORY DIDN'T *END* THERE. IN 1961, SHE WAS *MISSING*, HER NEW HUSBAND WAS *INCARCERATED* --"

"-- AND HER TWIN CHILDREN NEEDED *HELP* -- HELP ONLY *AUGUSTUS FURST* COULD PROVIDE."

"HE ADOPTED THEM, AND RAISED THEM AS HIS *OWN* --"

"-- AND WHAT WAS ONCE A TEAM OF *TWO* ADVENTURERS BECAME WORLD FAMOUS --"

"-- AS THE *FIRST FAMILY!*"

"BUT IT DIDN'T END *THERE*, EITHER. IN 1979, DR. FURST'S ADOPTIVE DAUGHTER *NATALIE* SHOCKED THE WORLD --"

"-- BY MARRYING *REX*, THE SON OF ONE OF THE FIRST FAMILY'S *GREATEST ENEMIES* --"

"-- AND IN 1986, THEIR *DAUGHTER* WAS BORN. THEIR DAUGHTER *ASTRA* --

"-- WHO'S NOW THE MOST *FAMOUS*, MOST *POWERFUL* TEN-YEAR-OLD GIRL IN THE WORLD --

-- AND OUR *GUEST* HERE IN THE STUDIO ON *"ASTRO KIDZ 2-DAY!"*

I'M YOUR *HOST*, STANLEY TRIPP, AND IT'S *GREAT* TO HAVE YOU HERE, ASTRA!

THANKS. IT WAS NICE OF YOU TO *INVITE* ME, MR. TRIPP.

GOTTA ASK -- DID YOUR *MOM* TELL YOU TO SAY THAT?

ASTRO KIDZ 2DAY

WITH STANLEY TRIPP

WELL... YEAH.

THAT'S THE WAY IT *IS* WITH MOMS, HUH? ALWAYS AFTER YOU TO MIND YOUR *MANNERS!*

SO, ASTRA, I'M SURE MOST OF THE KIDS IN OUR AUDIENCE ARE DYING TO *KNOW* --

-- DOES IT FEEL *WEIRD* TO TRAVEL TO OTHER DIMENSIONS AND FIGHT MONSTERS AND STUFF?

UM, NOT REALLY. IT'S *FUN*, BUT...

WHAT ABOUT BEING SO *FAMOUS* -- OR HAVING RELATIVES THAT AREN'T *HUMAN?* THAT'S *GOTTA* BE STRANGE!

I DON'T KNOW...I *GUESS*...

46

47

"-- WE'VE GOT AN *INTER-DIMENSIONAL BREAKOUT!*

SHOOM

IT'S THE *SILVER BRAIN* -- HE'S FOUND A WAY TO *RUPTURE* THE BOUNDARIES BETWEEN THE *MENTO-VERSE* AND *HERE* --

-- AND HE'S EMERGED AT THE UNIVERSITY *PSYCH LAB!*

EVERYONE PUT ON THESE *CEREBRA-CIRCUITS,* TO PROTECT YOU FROM HIS MENTAL DOMINATION.

UM, HE'S REALLY *SERGEI VLATAROFF,* A SCIENTIST WHO FIGURED OUT HOW TO GO ALL *MENTAL* -- AN' BECAME PURE *BRAIN.*

HE KEEPS TRYIN' TO *ENSLAVE* EVERYONE IN THE WORLD --

-- BUT LAST TIME HE DID, *SAMARITAN* THREW HIM INTO THE *MENTO-VERSE.*

AND *ASTRA* -- YOU'VE BEEN READING THE *FILES.* WHAT CAN YOU *TELL* US ABOUT THE SILVER BRAIN?

VERY GOOD. ANYTHING *ELSE?*

WELL, HE'S GOT NO *BODY,* SO HE'S ALWAYS GOT TO WORK THROUGH SOME KIND OF *UNDERLINGS...*

AN' *HOLY CATS,* LOOK WHO HE'S USING *THIS* TIME --

-- THE ANTI-BODIES!

ASTRA, YOU CAN'T JUST *BLAST THROUGH* THEM -- THEY'RE ENERGY-BEINGS *THEMSELVES* --

-- AND THEY CAN GRAB *HOLD* OF YOU!

Yeah, duh!

ZKAK ZKAK

SHOOM

ASTRA!

WE'LL GETCHA BACK, KID!

Uncle Nick an' Uncle Julie are the ones who've forgotten what the Anti-Bodies do.

They grab onto the energy-blasts, just like they do any loose energy -- take us all to the power core --

-- and stuff us in!

I can sense everybody **fighting** outside -- an' it feels like what Uncle Julie calls a "wild **ruckus**."

It seems like it goes on **forever**, but I've got **other** stuff to think about.

Maybe I don't know about **games**, an' I don't know about **sleepovers** and **TV shows** --

-- but I **do** know about energy.

I reach out, an' let myself **dissolve** a little into the energy core --

-- an' I find where the core's powering all of the Silver Brain's **stuff** --

-- an' I shut it all **off**.

HUH?

WHAT?!

THE DIMENSIONAL APERSTOMUM -- IT'S BEEN DE-ACTIVATED!

CLAK

TEK

59

C'MON, NICK, REX -- HELP ME GET THIS DINGUS INSIDE --

-- IT'LL MAKE A DANDY ADDITION TO THE TROPHY ROOM!

FINE, FINE. BUT WHEN YOU'RE DONE WITH THAT, JOIN ME IN LAB THREE --

-- WE'VE GOT TO SEAL OFF THE BREACH IN THE MENTO-VERSE -- PERMANENTLY!

UH, MOM?

CAN I ASK YOU A QUESTION?

YOU CAN ASK ME ANYTHING, ANYTIME, HONEY. YOU KNOW THAT. WHAT IS IT?

WELL, IT'S THIS GAME...

SURE. THAT'S CALLED "HOPSCOTCH."

"HOPSCOTCH." WHAT IS IT? HOW'S IT PLAYED?

YOU KNOW, I'M NOT REALLY SURE. I GREW UP WITH YOUR GRAMPA, SO I NEVER PLAYED IT AS A GIRL.

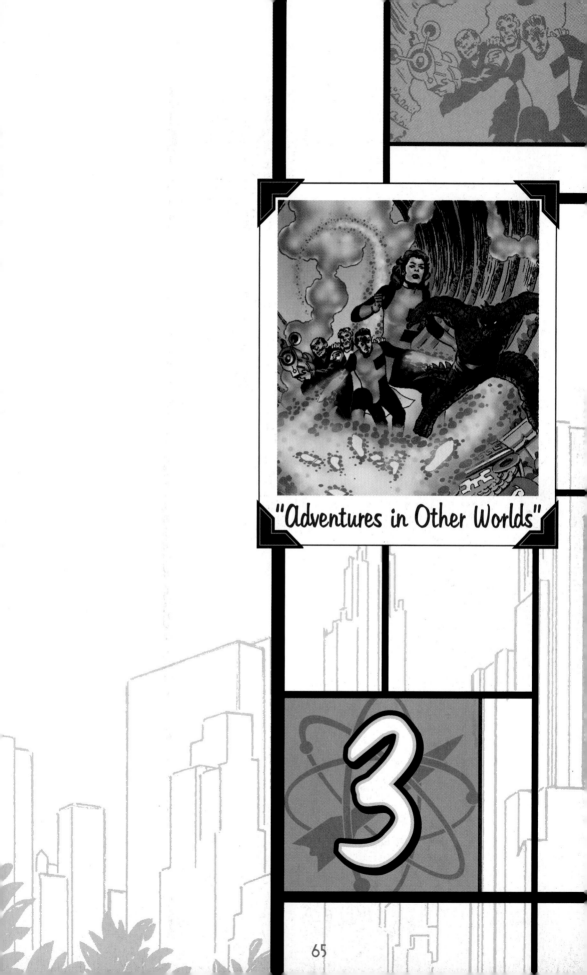

"Adventures in Other Worlds"

3

"-- AND I'M SURE YOU'LL ALL WANT TO MAKE HER FEEL *WELCOME.*"

WHAT DO YOU *MEAN,* MY GRANDDAUGHTER IS *MISSING?!*

NOW LOOK *HERE,* KASPIAN --

NO, AUGUSTUS FURST. *YOU* LOOK.

YOU TOOK *MY CHILDREN* FROM ME, AND RAISED THEM AS YOUR OWN. THAT MAY HAVE BEEN A *GOOD THING,* ALL IN ALL --

-- FOR SURELY, THEY WOULD HAVE HAD A *HARD* LIFE WITH THE *BEAST-PEOPLES.*

BUT THEY ARE STILL *BLOOD* OF MY *BLOOD,* AND TO HAVE THEM *TURNED* AGAINST ME, AS SO OFTEN YOU HAVE DONE --

-- IS MUCH INDEED TO *ENDURE.*

BUT NOW YOU TELL ME THAT ON *TOP* OF THIS, YOU'RE UNABLE TO SAFEGUARD A SINGLE *TEN-YEAR-OLD GIRL?*

HEY! ENOUGH WITH THE *MOUTH,* ALREADY!

YOU TALK *LOUDLY,* KASPIAN -- BUT WHAT ASSURANCES DO WE HAVE THAT *YOU* HAVEN'T TAKEN MY DAUGHTER?

REX, NO --

YOU... *DARE?*

73

SLAMM

YOU *DARE* ACCUSE *KASPIAN* OF THE *BEAST-MEN*?!

I AM A MAN OF *HONOR,* CREATURE! BAD ENOUGH YOU SULLY MY *DAUGHTER* WITH YOUR *TOUCH,* BUT TO --

-- NO. ENOUGH. I WILL SEND A MESSAGE THROUGH ALL THE TRIBES OF THE BEAST-MEN. ALL THE WILD WORLD WILL SEARCH FOR HER --

-- AND IF SHE CAN BE *FOUND* BY US, SHE *WILL* BE.

-- TAKE HIS *HEAD* OFF --

CALM *DOWN,* REX -- THIS *MINUTE!*

THANK YOU, KASPIAN. YOU DO US GREAT *SERVICE,* AND WE ARE *INDEBTED* TO YOU.

DO NOT *MISTAKE* ME, AUGUSTUS FURST. I DO NOT ACT IN *FRIENDSHIP.* I SEEK TO PROTECT BLOOD OF MY BLOOD -- -- AND NO *MORE.*

NOW GO --

75

I'M THE **BEST** HOPSCOTCH PLAYER AT *BOLLING ELEMENTARY SCHOOL,* THAT'S WHO I AM!

Everything happens kinda **fast** after that.

Someone calls **home** --

-- and they come get me.

And Mom's **mad,** like I thought --

-- but she **cries,** too.

And later --

"Show 'Em All"

4

Show 'Em All

THE *PSEUDO-GRAVITY INDUCTORS* IN THE SOLDIER'S FEET WORK *SPLENDIDLY*.

IT'S ACTUALLY *FUN*.

Etch - a - Sketch

IT TAKES *HOURS* TO HAUL IT ALL OUT. ONE ELDERLY MAN, WORKING ALONE -- OF *COURSE* IT DOES.

AND MY BACK WILL LET ME *KNOW* ABOUT IT, THE NEXT FEW DAYS.

BUT FINALLY, IT'S *DONE.* FINALLY, THE LAST TRIP IS *BEHIND* ME --

THE ACCESS HATCH IS CLOSED. ALL IS SECURE. THE ACCESS HATCH IS CLOSED. ALL IS SECURE.

-- AND ALL THAT REMAINS IS TO FLOAT IT DOWN TO THE *TRUCK.*

THE SUPERHEROES *STOPPED* ME, OF COURSE. PRIMARILY *JACK-IN-THE-BOX* -- HE STYMIED ME AT EVERY TURN.

BUT HE AND THE *OTHERS* WERE JUST HURDLES TO BE *OVERCOME.* I HAD TIME -- TIME AND MY *BRAIN* -- AND THAT'S ALL I *NEEDED.*

AND THIS TIME -- THIS TIME, IT'S *WORKED.* BY THE TIME THEY FINISH CATALOGUING WHAT'S *MISSING* --

-- I'VE GOT THE MONEY LAUNDERED AND TUCKED SAFELY AWAY IN A NUMBERED *GRAND CAYMAN* BANK ACCOUNT.

THEY'RE SCANNING THEIR DATABASES FOR MYTHICAL YOUNG, BRONZED HOLLYWOOD *TECHNO-CRIMINALS* --

-- AND I --

-- I'M STRAIGHTENING MY *SEAT-BACK* FOR THE DESCENT INTO *RIO DE JANEIRO.*

I CAN STILL TASTE THE *CHAMPAGNE* FROM MY COMPLIMENTARY *MIMOSA.*

AND RIO IS EVERYTHING IT *SHOULD* BE.

I STAY IN THE BEST HOTEL -- AND SPEND ENOUGH MONEY TO ATTRACT THE MOST SATISFYING OF COMPANIONS.

I SPEND MY DAYS IN THE SUN --

-- AND MY NIGHTS IN *SYBARITIC LUXURY* --

‹OH, LOOK -- THE *BIRDS OF PARADISE!* IT WAS ON THE RADIO EARLIER --

‹-- HOW THEY CAPTURED *SENHOR TECNICO!*›

‹THEY'RE SO *WONDERFUL* -- SO VIVACIOUS, SO *POWERFUL!* TO FLY LIKE THAT, TO FIGHT FOR *JUSTICE* --

‹-- IT MUST BE THE *GREATEST* THING IN THE *WORLD!*›

‹OH, THEY'RE NOT SO *SPECIAL...*›

-- THEY SHOULD BE JOYOUS, SHOULD BE EXPERIENCES TO BE *EMBRACED* --

-- TO BE REVELED IN AS MY *JUST REWARD* AFTER A *LIFETIME* OF TOIL.

BUT INSTEAD THEY FEEL LIKE -- LIKE *HIDING PLACES,* LIKE *REFUGES* AGAINST SOMETHING I'M *FLEEING.*

LIKE SHIELDS, LIKE *DISGUISES.* NOT LIKE DESTINATIONS *AT ALL.*

BUT THOSE CAPED, MASKED -- *LUNKHEADS!* THEY'RE MORONS! *FOOLS!* I OUTWITTED THEM *ALL* --

NOBODY KNOWS A

-- AND *NOBODY KNOWS A THING!*

BUT THEY DON'T SHAKE OFF THAT *EASILY* -- THEY'RE BUILT *NOT* TO.

AND THEIR NUMBERS *INCREASE* --

-- AND *INCREASE* --

-- AND IN THE END, I DON'T EVEN HAVE TO USE THE *SONIC INVERTER,* TO SHORT OUT HIS *POWER CONTAINMENT HARNESS.*

WHUMPP

THERE *IS* A TRICK TO DEFEATING THE ADHESION MARBLES -- THERE INVARIABLY IS.

PHYSICAL POWERS, *PHYSICAL* SOLUTIONS.

AND NO DOUBT, HE'LL HAVE FIGURED IT OUT BY THE TIME I HAVE TO USE THEM ON HIM *AGAIN.* BUT NOT *THIS* TIME.

THIS TIME, I GET TO A THIRD OF THE BANK'S AVAILABLE *CASH* BEFORE *CONVENTIONAL* AUTHORITIES ARRIVE.

AND WHILE THEY'RE TRYING TO FIGURE OUT HOW TO GET PAST *MY* SECURITY DEVICES, I TAKE MY *LEAVE* OF THEM.

THEY'RE STARTING TO PUT IT *TOGETHER.*

-- DARING TWILIGHT BATTLE BETWEEN THE *BLACK RAPIER* AND THE NOTORIOUS *JUNKMAN* --

THEY'VE REALIZED THE FIRST BANK WAS *MINE* -- AND THEY'RE EVEN STARTING TO FIGURE OUT HOW I *DID* IT.

EXTRA EDITION

Detroit Free Press
EXTRA EDITION

JUNKMAN ON CRIME SPREE?

Wary Banks Up Security

'M.O.' in AstroBank Heist is His As Well' S... Autho...

Oldster Eludes Speedster

Astro City Current

The AstroBank Robbery: First Clues Come to Ligh...

* The Man Who Counts the Crime...
* America's Most Powerful Schoo...
* Elementary Schoo... Report Card
* Restaurant R...

I CAN JUST PICTURE YOUNG *YUMIKO* -- YOU *SEE,* SENHOR, THEY WILL *CATCH* HIM NOW...

FOR THAT MATTER, THE MEDIA IS GIVING THE CREDIT TO THE *HEROES* --

-- EXCLUSIVE CAMCORDER FOOTAGE OF THE *NEW ORLEANS STANDOFF,* AND THE *BLACK RAPIER'S HEROIC* --

-- *M.P.H.* INTERRUPTS BANK ROBBERY, BLACK RAPIER THWARTS SUPERVILLAIN, YADDITA YADDITA *YADDITA.*

WHO'LL STOP THE *JUNKMAN'S* CRIME SPREE? *THAT'S* THEIR TACK. BUT THEY'LL *LEARN.* THEY'LL *ALL* LEARN.

THAT'S WHAT I'M *DOING* HERE, FIVE MONTHS TO THE DAY FROM WHEN I LEFT. THAT'S WHY I'M BACK IN *ASTRO CITY.*

THE *ASTROBANK TOWER* LOOKS MUCH THE SAME AS IT DID THE LAST TIME.

A FEW MORE *PIGEON DROPPINGS*, I'M SURE, SOME MORE WEATHERING -- BUT NOTHING I *NOTICE*.

I HAVE MUCH THE SAME *EQUIPMENT* AS LAST TIME. I'M FOLLOWING MUCH THE SAME *PLAN*.

I EVEN FIND THE SAME *ACCESS HATCH*. IT'S EASY TO TELL --

-- FROM THE *SCRATCHES* AND *SCRAPES* I LEFT GETTING IN BEFORE, AND AFTER *DETROIT*, AFTER THEY RECONSTRUCTED MY PATH --

-- I'M SURE *THEY* KNOW IT, TOO.

HEYA, JUNKMAN --

ASTRO

WITH MY SATCHEL, THEY MANAGE TO FIND MY *HEADQUARTERS*, MY *SUPPLIES* -- EVERYTHING BUT THE *MONEY*.

AND THEY'RE CONFIDENT THEY'LL FIND *THAT*, TOO, THEY SAY.

ASTRO CITY ◈ **ROCKET**

FRI NOV 21 1997

50¢ DAILY

JUNKMAN CAPTURED

Investigators Close to Full Recovery

Criminal's Lair Found in City

IT'S IN ALL THE *PAPERS*, LIKE BEFORE.

IT'S ON *TV*, TOO. BUT THIS TIME, THERE'S A *DIFFERENCE*.

-- NOTED *PSYCHIATRISTS* WILL TELL US *WHY* THE JUNKMAN DID IT -- AND ILLUMINATE HIS *FATAL FLAW* --

THIS TIME, THEY *KNOW* SOMETHING.

THEY DON'T KNOW *EVERYTHING*, OF COURSE -- THEY DON'T KNOW HOW I *MANAGED* IT, FOR INSTANCE.

THE POLICE ARE *WITHHOLDING* THAT, SAVING IT FOR THE TRIAL. AND *JACK-IN-THE-BOX* ISN'T TALKING, EITHER.

BUT THAT'S ALL RIGHT. IT'S COMING.

LADIES AND GENTLEMEN OF THE JURY, THE EVIDENCE YOU ARE ABOUT TO SEE --

-- WILL TAKE YOU *STEP BY STEP* THROUGH THE WORKINGS OF A BRILLIANT, BUT *DISTURBED* MIND --

COUNTY COURTHOUSE

-- AND PROVE BEYOND THE *SHADOW OF A DOUBT* THAT THIS MAN -- *THIS MAN* -- SINGLEHANDEDLY COMMITTED THE CRIMES HE'S --

BLAH BLAH *BLAH.* THE PROSECUTOR IS THE *BEST* THEY'VE GOT, THE *TY COBB* OF DISTRICT ATTORNEYS.

MY LAWYER, ON THE OTHER HAND, IS A SCARED LITTLE *KITTEN,* THE INK STILL WET ON HIS CREDENTIALS. NO *COMPETITION.*

SO THE GREAT MAN, THE *GOLDEN ORATOR* -- HE'S GOING TO TELL EVERYONE *EXACTLY* WHAT I DID, AND EXACTLY *HOW.*

AND THEY'RE GOING TO DRINK IN EVERY *WORD,* EVERY *INVENTION,* EVERY EXHIBIT, EVERY STROKE OF *GENIUS.*

AND THEN THE PROSECUTION WILL *REST.* AND I'LL TRIGGER MY *ESCAPE PLAN,* WHICH HAS BEEN IN PLACE FOR *DAYS.*

I'LL *LEAVE* -- AND THEY'LL HAVE THAT MUCH MORE TO TALK ABOUT, *EH?* MEANWHILE, I FEEL THEIR *EYES* ON ME, FASCINATED.

BUT THERE'S NOT MUCH FOR ME TO *DO,* NOT AT THE MOMENT. NOT MUCH, EXCEPT TO *SMILE* FOR THE SKETCH ARTISTS.

IT SHOULD BE A *DELIGHTFUL* SHOW.

YOU ARE NOW LEAVING ASTRO CITY PLEASE DRIVE CAREFULLY

"Serpent's Teeth"

I GUESS THAT'S HOW IT *IS* WITH JACK-IN-THE-BOX, *EH*, GORDON? HE ALWAYS *BOUNCES BACK.*

HA-HA! AND I THOUGHT *MY* JOKES WERE BAD, TAMRA.

I'M *GORDON MEADOWS* WITH *TAMRA DIXON,* FOR *KBAC-3,* WISHING YOU THE *BEST* OF EVENINGS.

MADE IT *AGAIN,* ZACK. MADE IT *AGAIN...*

I CATCH THE *NEWSCAST,* LIKE I ALMOST ALWAYS HAVE SINCE SHE GOT MOVED UP TO *EVENINGS.*

AND I CATCH HER RELIEVED *SMILE* AT THE SIGN-OFF, AND CAN'T HELP BUT SMILE BACK, EVEN THOUGH I KNOW SHE CAN'T *SEE* IT.

MADE IT *AGAIN,* TAMRA.

YOU GOING TO GO OVER SCHEMATICS ALL *NIGHT,* Z.J.? THEY'LL STILL BE HERE *TOMORROW,* YOU KNOW --

-- AND THAT PRETTY *WIFE* OF YOURS'LL BE ON HER WAY *HOME* ALREADY...

WHEN YOU'RE *RIGHT,* JACINDA, YOU'RE RIGHT. I THINK I KNOW HOW TO FIX THAT *SHOULDER ASSEMBLY* -- BUT IT'LL WAIT.

I'LL SEE YOU IN THE *MORNING.* YOU AND CRASH HAVE YOURSELF THE *BEST* OF EVENINGS, YOU HEAR?

OH, *YOU.* TAKING THE *SUBWAY?* WE HEAD THE SAME DIRECTION...

NOT TONIGHT, JACE. I'VE GOT SOME *ERRANDS* TO RUN. *CATCH* YOU NEXT TIME, THOUGH.

I DON'T HAVE ANY *ERRANDS,* OF COURSE. IT'S JUST, WELL --

AND ON I GO, VAULTING, LEAPING, AND THE ROOFS OF *GAINESVILLE* COME INTO VIEW --

-- AND I'M *SMILING* AGAIN, AS BROADLY AS MY *MASK*. I'M A HAPPY MAN, I GUESS --

-- A *HAPPY MAN*.

ONE QUICK CHANGE IN THE ALLEY'S *SHADOWS*, AND...

HOW'S ASTRO CITY'S *HOTTEST* NEWS PERSONALITY?

ZACK!

YOU KNOW FULL WELL I'M LIKE NUMBER *FIVE* OR *SOMETHING*.

OH, I WASN'T *TALKING* ABOUT Q-RATINGS...

WELL, THEN.

AND HOW ARE THE ROBOT *DOGS* COMING, HM?

THAT'S *ROBODOGS*. AND I THINK THE LAST *GLITCH* IS SOLVED -- WE'LL BE ABLE TO ROLL 'EM OUT AT *TOYFAIR*.

BUT WHO WANTS TO TALK ABOUT *BUSINESS*, ANYWAY?

ZACHARY JOHNSON, I'M HUNGRY AND I'M *TIRED*. AND I RENTED A *VIDEO*.

I'LL RUB YOUR *BACK*...

YOUR SON. YOU DIED BEFORE I WAS BORN, THOUGH. DIED WITHOUT PREPARING ME -- WITHOUT *TRAINING* ME.

I DIDN'T KNOW THE LEGACY I CARRIED UNTIL I WAS TWELVE. ALL THAT TIME, ALL THOSE YEARS -- LOST!

"BUT I CHOSE TO LIVE UP TO YOUR EXAMPLE NONETHELESS -- TO LIVE UP TO MY HERITAGE!

"I HAD MYSELF *CYBERNETICALLY* ALTERED, TO AUGMENT MY PHYSICAL ABILITIES, TO GIVE ME THE EDGE I NEEDED."

YOU -- MUTILATED YOURSELF?

I DID! AND I HAVE -- REBUILDING AND IMPROVING MYSELF FURTHER AND FURTHER AS I NEEDED MORE *POWER!*

I WOULD HAVE DONE *ANYTHING* TO FOLLOW IN YOUR FOOTSTEPS!

"I MADE MYSELF COLD. I MADE MYSELF HARD, AND BRUTAL -- JUDGE AND JURY IN THE WAR AGAINST *CRIME!*

"BUT IT WAS NOT *ENOUGH!* I WAS OVERWHELMED -- CRIME COULD NOT BE STEMMED. AND THEN I REALIZED --

YOU -- YOU CAN'T BASE A *RELIGION* ON OFF-THE-CUFF JOKES... *CAN* YOU?

YOU... *FORSWEAR* YOUR OWN *WORDS?*

YOU SPIT ON THE VERY *BUILDING BLOCKS* OF MY *CREED?* YOU CALL THE SACRED WORDS A *JOKE?!*

YOU ARE *NOT* THE JACK -- AND I SHOULD *NOT* HAVE SAVED YOU! YOU ARE AN *IMPOSTER,* A *TRAVESTY,* A *LIE!* AND FOR YOUR *CALUMNY* -- -- YOU MUST *DIE!*

FOR THE *FIRST TIME,* YOU *FREAKISH ABERRATION* --

-- YOU SAY SOMETHING I CAN *AGREE* WITH. WE WILL JOIN FORCES, THEN -- UNTIL OUR *PROGENITOR* HAS PAID FOR HIS CRIMES.

THEN WE CAN SETTLE OUR *OWN* DIFFERENCES.

DEPUTIZED! DEPUTIZED!

AND AS A POINT OF PROCEDURE, *FATHER DEAR,* DON'T ATTEMPT TO *ELECTROCUTE* CYBORGS. IT ONLY *BOOSTS* THEIR POWER.

THEY COME *FORWARD,* THEN -- SHOULDER TO SHOULDER, WITH THE SAME FLAT, COLD *LOOK* IN THEIR EYES.

AND I'M STILL NOT BELIEVING ANY OF IT. I NEED TIME TO *THINK.* TIME --

I WAIT UNTIL THE *COPS* ARRIVE, THEN WAIT FURTHER, WHILE THEY CALL IN THE *SPECIAL INCARCERATION* SQUAD.

JACKSON *THAWS OUT*, BUT BY THEN THEY'VE GOT HIM IN A JURY-RIGGED *CAGE*.

AND THE WHOLE TIME, NEITHER OF THEM *SAY* ANYTHING. THEY JUST *STARE* AT ME WITH BALEFUL, HATE-FILLED EYES.

MY *BOYS.* I *BELIEVE* IT NOW -- OR AT LEAST I BELIEVE IT *COULD* BE TRUE. IT SURE *FEELS* REAL.

AND -- IF IT'S A *SCAM* -- WHO WOULD KNOW...

FINALLY, I CAN *GO.* AND I TELL MYSELF I DON'T HAVE TO *THINK* ABOUT IT. I DON'T *HAVE* ANY KIDS. TAMRA AND I *TALKED* ABOUT IT, BUT THAT'S ALL.

ALL I WANT -- *ALL* I WANT --

-- IS *HOME.*

I HEARD ABOUT IT ON THE NEWS -- ABOUT *SOME* OF IT ANYWAY. WHAT *HAPPENED?*

LATER, OKAY? I'LL TELL YOU *LATER.*

6

"Father's Day"

"HE WAS A DESIGNER FOR *WHAMCO TOYS.* A BLACK DESIGNER IN THE EARLY SIXTIES WAS *UNUSUAL,* BUT HE WAS TALENTED --

"-- SO THEY *HIRED* HIM, AND PAID HIM HALF WHAT LESS PRODUCTVE *WHITE* DESIGNERS MADE.

"BUT THEN, BY *CHANCE,* HE DISCOVERED THAT SOME OF HIS TOY DESIGNS WERE BEING USED IN *WEAPONS* --

"-- *WEAPONS* USED BY THE *UNDERWORLD.*

"HE TRIED TO GET TO THE BOTTOM OF IT AT *WHAMCO,* BUT ALL THAT HAPPENED WAS THAT HE GOT *FIRED.*

"STILL, HE DIDN'T LET IT GO. HE TRIED TO FIND THE *LINK* BETWEEN WHAMCO AND THE MOBS -- TRIED TO *EXPOSE* IT.

"NOBODY *BELIEVED* HIM, BUT WHAMCO WANTED HIM TO *SHUT UP* ANYWAY.

"SO THEY HAD HIS FATHER -- MY *GRANDFATHER* -- KIDNAPPED.

"THAT'S WHEN HE CUSTOMIZED SOME OF HIS *TOY DESIGNS,* WORKED UP A COSTUME --

"-- AND BECAME *JACK-IN-THE-BOX* -- FIRST TO RESCUE MY GRANDFATHER, AND THEN TO CONTINUE HIS *INVESTIGATION.*

"HE TOOK ON THE *MOBS,* HE TOOK ON *WHAMCO,* AND EVENTUALLY HE EXPOSED THEM. HE *WON.*

"BUT HE STILL KEPT *FIGHTING* -- FOR OTHERS WHO'D BEEN VICTIMIZED, WHO NEEDED *HELP.* HE'D BECOME A *HERO.*

"AND THEN ON *OCTOBER 13, 1983* --

"-- HE *DIED*, KILLED IN AN EXPLOSION WHILE FIGHTING MINIONS OF THE *UNDERLORD*.

"BUT HE TOOK THE *UNDERLORD* DOWN, TOO -- OR SO IT SEEMED. HE DIED *SAVING* PEOPLE. MAKING THE WORLD A *BETTER PLACE*.

"ME, I WAS TWELVE. AND I DIDN'T KNOW *ANY* OF THIS.

"BUT I FOLLOWED IN MY FATHER'S *FOOTSTEPS* -- STUDYING *ENGINEERING*, DESIGNING TOYS OF *MY OWN* --

"-- AND WHEN I WAS EIGHTEEN, MY *MOTHER* DIED TOO. AND IN THE PROCESS OF SETTLING THE ESTATE --

"-- I FOUND MY FATHER'S *GADGETS* AND *JOURNALS*. I FOUND THE *TRUTH*.

"THERE WAS A *LOT* IN THOSE JOURNALS -- *INCLUDING* THE UNDERLORD'S TRUE IDENTITY. AND HE *WASN'T* DEAD.

"MY MOTHER EITHER NEVER *KNEW*, OR SHE THOUGHT I WAS TOO YOUNG TO KNOW. SO I DIDN'T GET *TOLD*.

"I BECAME THE *SECOND* JACK-IN-THE-BOX THEN. TO BRING IN THE UNDERLORD, TO GET *JUSTICE* FOR MY FATHER.

Veidt H.

"AND BY THE TIME I *MANAGED* THAT --

"-- I STAYED IN COSTUME, LIKE *HE* HAD. I BECAME A SUPERHERO, TOO.

YOU *KNOW* ALL THAT. I'VE TOLD IT A DOZEN TIMES. BUT THERE'S MORE *TO* IT. THERE'S A PART I'VE NEVER REALLY *TALKED* ABOUT.

THAT'S THE PART ABOUT WHAT IT'S LIKE TO BE TWELVE YEARS OLD AND HAVE YOUR FATHER JUST... *VANISH.*

"I DIDN'T KNOW WHAT HAD *HAPPENED.* MY MOM SAID HE WAS DEAD, BUT THERE WAS NO BODY, NO *FUNERAL.*

"WAS HE *REALLY* DEAD? OR WAS HE JUST *GONE?* DID HE LEAVE -- DID HE JUST NOT *LOVE* US? I DIDN'T KNOW.

"I CAME UP WITH ALL KINDS OF FANTASIES -- HE WAS A *SPY,* OR AN *UNDERCOVER COP.* OR IN THE *WITNESS PROTECTION PROGRAM.*

"SOMETIMES, I EVEN IMAGINED HE WAS A DARING *CRIMINAL MASTERMIND,* ON THE RUN FROM THE LAW. *STUPID,* HUH?

"BUT THE BOTTOM LINE WAS, HE WAS *GONE.* AND I SPENT SIX YEARS TRYING TO *FILL* THAT HOLE --

"-- TRYING TO WIN THE APPROVAL OF A *GHOST,* TO BE WHAT MY FATHER WOULD HAVE WANTED WITHOUT KNOWING WHAT THAT *WAS.*

"AND IN THE END, WHEN I LEARNED THAT THE TRUTH EXCEEDED *ALL* MY FANTASIES, I WAS *PROUD,* AND I WAS HONORED --

"-- BUT STILL, THERE WAS A PART OF ME THAT FELT *HOLLOW* --

"-- THAT FELT LIKE MY FATHER HAD CARED MORE ABOUT *FIGHTING CRIME* THAN ABOUT HIS *FAMILY.*"

FINGER STREET PRECINCT STATION.

DETECTIVE WILLIAMS LETS ME IN, TO WHERE THEY'RE BEING HELD FOR *PROCESSING*, BEFORE THEY'RE MOVED TO *BIRO ISLAND*.

I *LOOK* AT THEM, AND I DON'T KNOW WHAT TO THINK.

ARE THEY MY SONS -- SOMETHING THAT MY CHILDREN COULD *BECOME*, IN SOME WARPED FUTURE?

COULD THIS REALLY *HAPPEN?* IF I DIED, COULD THE CHILD GROWING INSIDE TAMRA BECOME -- SOMETHING LIKE *THAT?*

IS THAT REALLY ALL I'VE GOT TO *GIVE* TO MY FAMILY -- PAIN, AND A TWISTED, HARMFUL *LEGACY?*

IS IT?

YOU MUST BE JUDGED, FATHER. JUDGED FOR FAILING YOUR SON. FOR FAILING YOUR *WORLD.*

YOU ARE A *HERETIC* AND A *FALSE PROPHET*, BLIND TO YOUR OWN TEACHINGS. YOU WILL BE *CLEANSED.*

151

152

TAMRA TOLD ME ONCE THAT WATCHING ME ON *TV* MUST BE WHAT IT'S LIKE FOR *FOOTBALL WIVES* --

-- IF THE OPPOSING TEAM HAD *UZIS.*

OKAY, GORILLA BOYS -- YOU'RE GOIN' *DOWN!*

YOU BEEN THROWIN' ME *AROUND* SOME --

BUT *THIS* TIME, AS SHE TELLS ME AFTERWARD, HER FIRST THOUGHT IS, *"DID THEY DRUG HIM?"* RIGHT FROM HER FIRST GLIMPSE --

-- LET'S SEE HOW YOU LIKE GETTING *THROWN* --

-- *HUH?*

-- YOU OUGHTTA KNOW THAT BY NOW!

OUR MASKS COME OFF, CLOWN --

WHAM
KRAM
BRAM

WHUDD
THUDD

-- SHE KNOWS SOMETHING'S WRONG.

ZACK -- YOU *KNOW* HOW TO FIGHT THESE GUYS! C'MON, ZACK -- YOU CAN *DO* THIS!

159

"THAT'S ROSCOE. ROSCOE JAMES."

OKAY, BRASS MONKEY --

-- NOW IT'S YOUR TURN!

I REALIZED I WAS LOOKING AT THE PROJECT BACKWARDS.

I WASN'T WILLING TO RISK LOSING OUR BABY HIS FATHER -- BUT JACK-IN-THE-BOX WAS NEEDED, TOO.

SO, WELL, WE CAN'T GET THE BABY A NEW FATHER, BUT WHAT ABOUT THE OTHER SIDE OF THE EQUATION?

WHAT ABOUT A NEW JACK-IN-THE-BOX?

A NEW -- ?

NO, ROSCOE!

"DON'T UNDERESTIMATE HIM!"

SO, LITTLE GUY -- -- YOU'RE NOT SO TOUGH --

165

"In the Spotlight"

7

JOSS RYERSON Account Exec

Paul ARTHUR ADVERTISING

AstroBank Tower
Suite 1300
Astro City

"-- AND IT DIDN'T TAKE LONG TO FIGURE OUT THAT THE SHORT HAIRY FELLOW WAS *BEHIND* IT ALL --"

HA! GET HIM, KORRGA! MUSS HIS *COIF!*

"-- AND, WELL, THE FELLOW IN THE TUXEDO SEEMED LIKE A *NICE* ENOUGH GUY --"

"-- SO --"

SHOULD YOU REALLY BE *PLAYING* WITH THIS?

HEY!

QUICK, SMASH THE *RAY!* WITHOUT IT, THE GORILLA CAN'T *EXIST!* QUICKLY --

-- *SMASH* IT!

"SO I *DID.*"

KSSH

"SURE ENOUGH, THE MONSTER BEGAN TO *FADE AWAY* --"

"AND TO MY *SHOCK* --"

WH- *WHAT* --?

177

"IT WAS THE GENTLEMAN WHO *RESCUED* ME. HE REALIZED WHAT MUST HAVE *HAPPENED* --"

I FEEL SO -- SO *STRANGE* --

PEOPLE! PEOPLE, *LISTEN* TO ME!

THIS MAN, THIS -- WELL, THIS *LION* -- JUST *SAVED YOU ALL!*

AND HE *WOULDN'T* HAVE BEEN HERE TO *DO* IT -- WOULDN'T HAVE BEEN HERE AT *ALL* --

-- IF PROFESSOR BORZOI'S *BELIEF RAY* HADN'T BROUGHT HIM TO LIFE, USING *YOUR* BELIEF IN HIM!

AND NOW HE'S *DYING!* HE SACRIFICED THE THING THAT BROUGHT HIM TO LIFE -- TO SAVE *YOU!* BUT YOU CAN SAVE *HIM,* IN TURN --

-- IF YOU'LL ONLY *BELIEVE!*

BELIEVE IN HIM! BELIEVE HE'S *REAL!* IT'S THE ONLY THING THAT'LL *SAVE HIM!*

"IT WAS A GOOD IMPULSE. A *GENEROUS* IMPULSE. BUT THE GENTLEMAN'S *ALWAYS* BEEN LIKE THAT.

"HE DIDN'T THINK IT THROUGH. HE JUST *ACTED* -- JUST STIRRED THE CROWD INTO *BELIEVING* IN ME --"

WH- *WHAT...?*

"-- AND THAT'S HOW ALL MY TROUBLES *BEGAN.*

"FIRST THERE WAS THE *COURT CASE.* I'D STUCK AROUND -- HAD A FEW *ADVENTURES* WITH THE GENTLEMAN --

"-- WHEN I HEARD FROM THE STUDIO'S *LAWYERS,* CLAIMING THAT THEY'D MADE ME UP -- SO I WAS THEIR *PROPERTY.*

"-- GOTTEN IN THE *NEWS* A LITTLE --

"WELL, THEY SHOULD HAVE MADE UP SOMEONE MORE *TRACTABLE.* I DIDN'T *LIKE* IT, AND NEITHER DID THE GENT --

"-- SO HE FOUND ME A *LAWYER,* AND WE WERE GOING TO FIGHT IT. WE'D PROBABLY HAVE *LOST* --

"-- THIS WAS THE *FORTIES,* AND ARTIFICIAL BEINGS WEREN'T *AROUND* MUCH, NOT LIKE NOW --

"-- BUT I HAD A REPUTATION AS A *POCKET HERO,* YOU KNOW -- AND THE STUDIOS DIDN'T WANT THE BAD *PUBLICITY* --

"-- THEY DIDN'T WANT TO SEEM LIKE *BAD* GUYS, ENSLAVING A PUBLIC CELEBRITY WHO'D SAVED *LIVES.*

"THEY OFFERED ME A *DEAL* -- THEY'D GET THE RIGHTS TO MY *EXISTING* CARTOONS IN PERPETUITY --

"-- BUT THEY'D HAVE NO CLAIM ON *ME.* AND THEY EVEN OFFERED ME A *CONTRACT,* FOR FEATURES."

AGREEMENT

"SO WE *SETTLED* OUT OF COURT.

FEATURES!

"DAZED AT THE OFFER, I *TOOK* IT.

"AND THE FEATURES DID *BOFFO.*

"WHY, WHEN *FRANCIS THE TALKING MULE* CAME ALONG IN '49 -- THEY COULDN'T *TOUCH* US.

"STARS WERE *LINING UP* TO DO CAMEOS IN MY PICTURES -- THEIR KIDS WOULDN'T *LET* 'EM TURN US DOWN.

"I WAS THE *TOAST* OF THE TOWN. I WAS INVITED TO *ALL* THE RIGHT PARTIES, POPULAR WITH *WOMEN* --"

LEO, *DAAAAARLING!*

"-- IN THE *COLUMNS* ALL THE TIME --"

THIS WAY, KIDS! SAY 'SIRLOIN!'

"IT WAS ALL ONE BIG MAD WHIRL OF *FLASHBULBS* AND *CHAMPAGNE.* I HAD IT GREAT, AND I *KNEW* IT --

"-- I HAD *EVERYTHING* --

"-- EVERYTHING I COULD EVER *WANT.*"

"BUT THE FILMS WERE A *GIMMICK,* AND AFTER A WHILE, *ALL* GIMMICKS GET OLD.

"BY 1954, NOBODY WAS *COMING* ANY MORE.

PANAMA LEO

"AND IT WASN'T LIKE I COULD MOVE OVER TO *BOGART* ROLES, OR EVEN *DANNY KAYE* STUFF.

"THERE WAS SOME TALK OF A REMAKE OF 'THE *WIZARD OF OZ,'* BUT THAT CAME TO *NOTHING.*

"MY *CONTRACT* CAME UP. AND THE STUDIO DIDN'T *RENEW.*

"I WAS WORRIED I'D *FADE AWAY* -- THAT WHEN THE AUDIENCES FORGOT ME, I'D *VANISH.* BUT I *DIDN'T.*

"I'D BEEN *AROUND* LONG ENOUGH, I GUESS. ENOUGH PEOPLE HAD BELIEVED IN ME TO MAKE ME *REAL.*

I EVEN REMEMBER THINKING HOW *LUCKY* I WAS, TO BE ALIVE FOR REAL. CAN YOU *BELIEVE* IT?

"I FOUND A JOB IN *TELEVISION.* HOSTING A *KIDDIE SHOW* SHOT OUT OF BURBANK.

"THERE WASN'T MUCH *MONEY,* BUT HEY -- IT WAS *WORK,* RIGHT?

FUN-TIME FARM

NBC

"AND THE *KIDS* SEEMED TO LIKE IT, AND IT KEPT A *ROOF* OVER MY HEAD --

"-- BUT THE MERRY-GO-ROUND RIDE WAS *OVER*. I GUESS I SHOULD HAVE BEEN HAPPY IT LASTED AS LONG AS IT *DID*.

"BEFORE YOU KNEW IT, PEOPLE I THOUGHT WERE MY *BOSOM BUDDIES* WEREN'T HOME WHEN I CALLED --

"-- AND THEY NEVER GOT AROUND TO *CALLING BACK* --

"-- AND FOR THE FIRST TIME, I HAD TIME TO *THINK* -- TO REALIZE HOW LITTLE I HAD.

"I WASN'T *ALIVE* UNTIL '46, BUT I WAS BORN WITH THE MEMORIES OF THE *CARTOONS* I'D BEEN IN --

"-- OF THE *ADVENTURES*, OF CHASTE ROMANCE WITH *LIONESS LOLA* --

"-- OF MY *RASCALLY NEPHEWS* --

"BUT ALL THEY WERE WERE *MEMORIES* --

"-- AND *FICTIONAL* ONES, AT THAT.

"I GOT INTO *TROUBLE* AFTER THAT -- *DRINKING* TOO MUCH, LOOSE WOMEN IN *BARS* --

"-- JUST GENERALLY *MIXING* IT UP.

"THE COPS SWEPT IT UNDER THE *RUG*, THOUGH --

"-- THEY *DID* THAT FOR CELEBRITIES IN THOSE DAYS. EVEN *HAS-BEENS*."

SLEEP IT *OFF*, WOULDJA, MR. *LEO?* MY BOY WATCHES YOUR *SHOW* --

-- AN' I WOULDN'T WANT HIM T'BE *DISAPPOINTED*.

YOUR *BOY*, OFFICER?

WOULD HE LIKE AN *AUTOGRAPH?*

"STILL, THERE WASN'T A RUG *BIG ENOUGH* TO SWEEP IT UNDER WHEN *CORLISS McBRIDE* DIED.

"OH, *I* DIDN'T KILL HER -- NOT DIRECTLY, ANYWAY. SHE WAS A *HOOKER* --

"-- SHE OD'D IN THE *MOONGLOW*, A CHEAP HOTEL THAT WAS MORE *BORDELLO* AND *BAR* THAN ANYTHING ELSE.

"THE MOONGLOW WAS PRACTICALLY MY *SECOND HOME* BACK THEN -- AND CORLISS, WHO I KNEW AS *TRIXIE* --

"-- SHE WAS THE *CLOSEST* THING I HAD TO A *FRIEND*.

"AND EVEN *SHE* WOULDN'T'VE HUNG AROUND, IF NOT FOR THE *MONEY* I GAVE HER, AND THE *DOPE* SHE *BOUGHT* WITH IT."

183

Oh, AND IT TURNED OUT LITTLE CORLISS HAD A *SECRET.*

SHE WAS *FOURTEEN* YEARS OLD.

"I WAS THE ONE WHO *FOUND* HER, AND THE POLICE LOOKED AT ME JUST LIKE *ANYONE ELSE.*

"BUT I *WASN'T* ANYONE ELSE, WAS I?"

"THERE WAS A *SCANDAL.* IT WAS IN THE *PAPERS,* COAST TO COAST --

Los Angeles Times EXTRA

February 7, 1957

KIDDIE TV STAR INVOLVED IN TEENYBOPPER DRUG DEATH

"He Killed Her For His Depr... Ple...

"-- AND CORLISS'S *MOTHER* TURNED UP FROM OHIO, DEMANDING I BE PUT IN *JAIL.*

"THERE WAS A BOOK LATER -- IT SEEMS CORLISS'S DEAR MA *BEAT* HER, WHICH IS WHY SHE RAN OFF IN THE *FIRST PLACE* --

"-- BUT THAT DIDN'T *MATTER* BACK THEN. IT MADE GOOD *HEADLINES,* IS WHAT MATTERED.

SHE WAS A *GOOD KID,* TRIXIE. I LIKE TO THINK IF I'D KNOWN, I COULD HAVE *DONE* SOMETHING, *HELPED* MAYBE.

BUT THAT'S A *CROCK.* MAYBE I DIDN'T KILL HER, BUT I SURE *HELPED* PUT THAT NEEDLE IN HER ARM --

-- AND WOULD IT *REALLY* HAVE MADE IT BETTER IF SHE WAS AN *EIGHTEEN-YEAR-OLD* JUNKIE CORPSE?

"THE GRAND JURY DECIDED NOT TO *INDICT* ME.

"NO EVIDENCE THAT *ANYONE* IN THE MOONGLOW HAD DONE WORSE THAN LOOK THE *OTHER WAY* --

"-- WHICH IS *BAD ENOUGH*, COME TO THAT. JUST NOT *ILLEGAL*.

"MY *CAREER*, OF COURSE, WAS AS DEAD AS *SHE* WAS.

"NOBODY WANTED AN ACCUSED *CHILD-KILLER* HOSTING A KIDDIE SHOW, AND WHO COULD *BLAME* THEM?

"AND THERE WAS *SOMETHING ELSE*, TOO.

"THERE WAS SOMETHING IN PEOPLE'S *EYES*, WHEN THEY LOOKED AT ME, SOMETHING *NEW*.

"IT WAS SOMETHING *HARSH*, AND COLD --

"-- AND IT WAS SOMETHING I'D *EARNED*.

"SO OUT I WENT, *AWAY* FROM IT ALL, AWAY FROM *EVERYTHING*.

"SO LONG, *HOLLYWOOD*.

"THERE'S AN *ADVANTAGE* TO BEING A CARTOON CHARACTER, ONE I'D NEVER *DISCOVERED* UNTIL THEN.

"MAYBE YOU GET HUNGRY, BUT YOU DON'T *NEED* TO *EAT,* NOT REALLY.

"SLEEP IN THE *RAIN,* FREEZE IN THE *COLD,* WALK THIS COUNTRY FROM *ONE* END TO THE *OTHER* --

"-- YOU WON'T *DIE.*

"NOT EVEN IF YOU DO IT FOR *SIX YEARS* -- IF NO ONE'LL HIRE YOU EVEN TO *WASH DISHES.*

"I BEGAN TO PRAY FOR *DEATH,* FOR RELEASE FROM THE GNAWING EMPTINESS, THE COLD, THE *PAIN.*

"BUT IT DIDN'T *COME.*

"I WAS HUDDLED ON A CLIFF IN THE ROCKIES, WONDERING IF *WILD ANIMALS* COULD TEAR ME APART OR SOMETHING --

"-- WONDERING IF EVEN *THAT* WOULD END IT --

"-- WHEN *ZZARDO* FOUND ME."

"ZZARDO HAD TOLD ME I WAS A *'BELIEF-FOCUS,'* THAT I SOAKED UP PSYCHIC ENERGY JUST BY *EXISTING.*

"HE WAS LYING ABOUT THAT *SECOND* PART, OF COURSE. HE JUST WANTED ME TO KILL *HONOR GUARD* FOR HIM. NOT THAT IT *MATTERED.*

"HE SAID I COULD *DRAIN* IT AWAY -- *KILLING* ME, SENDING ME BACK WHERE I *BELONGED,* WHATEVER.

"I DID THE *DIALOGUE* OKAY, BUT I COULDN'T PLAY THE *ROLE,* NOT FULLY. SO EVEN IF HE'D BEEN TELLING THE *TRUTH,* IT WOULDN'T HAVE HAPPENED.

"THE SILVER AGENT AND THE OTHERS WERE *SYMPATHETIC,* BUT STILL, THERE WAS GOING TO BE A *TRIAL* --

"-- UNTIL MY OLD PALS AT THE *STUDIO* STEPPED IN, THAT IS.

"*FAGO'S FUNNY FEATURES* WAS A PART OF *OMNIVERSAL PICTURES,* BY THEN --

"-- AND THEY'D BEEN MAKING GOOD MONEY WITH THEIR CARTOONS ON *TV* -- RERUNS, LICENSING, THE *WORKS.*

"EVERYTHING BUT THE *LOONY LEO* SHORTS, THAT IS. AND THEY WANTED TO SHOW *THOSE,* TOO --

"-- WANTED TO BRING 'EM OUT AS SOON AS PEOPLE HAD *FORGOTTEN* ABOUT CORLISS McBRIDE --

"-- AND THEY DIDN'T WANT *ANOTHER* SCANDAL DREDGING IT UP *ALL OVER* AGAIN.

"*HONOR GUARD* WAS WILLING TO GIVE ME ANOTHER *CHANCE,* AND SOME MONEY CROSSED THE RIGHT *PALMS* IN OUR FINE JUSTICE SYSTEM --

"-- AND LIKE *THAT,* IT ALL

"SOME MONEY CROSSED *MY* PAW, TOO. THE STUDIO DIDN'T WANT ME TURNING UP IN THE *PAPERS,* AFTER ALL --

"-- DIDN'T WANT ONE OF THEIR STARS TO SURFACE AS A *HOMELESS BUM.*

"SO THEY SET ME UP WITH A *STAKE,* AND IT WAS ENOUGH TO KEEP ME *GOING.*

"I BOUGHT A HOUSE IN *GOLDWATER HEIGHTS,* ON THE OUTSKIRTS OF *ASTRO CITY --*

"-- AND I DIDN'T GO *OUT* MUCH.

HOUSE FOR SALE

"THE HOUSE WAS EVENTUALLY THOUGHT TO BE *HAUNTED,* AND WHEN I *DID* GO OUT... IT WASN'T PLEASANT."

YAHH!
YAHH!

"THE KIDS HAD NO IDEA WHO I *WAS,* OF COURSE --

"-- THEY WERE JUST TERRORIZING THE NEIGHBORHOOD *FREAK.*

"AND THEN, IN *1976*, THEY STARTED SHOWING MY CARTOONS ON *TV* AGAIN. THE PAST, IT SEEMED, WAS FINALLY *PAST*.

"I WOULD *WATCH* THEM, AND TELL MYSELF THAT PART OF MY LIFE WAS OVER, AND THAT I WAS *BETTER OFF* FOR IT.

"BUT A FEW YEARS *LATER*, I WAS APPROACHED BY SOME BUSINESSMEN. *ENTREPRENEURS*.

"THEY'D TRACKED ME DOWN, FOUND OUT WHERE I *LIVED*.

"THEY WANTED TO OPEN A *RESTAURANT*, A FORTIES NOSTALGIA PLACE. AND THEY WANTED TO BUILD IT AROUND *ME* --

"-- TO MAKE ME A LIVING *PROMOTIONAL GIMMICK*.

"THEY LAID IT ALL *OUT* FOR ME, HOW IT WOULD *WORK*.

"THERE WAS ONLY ONE *HITCH*..."

WE NEED YOU TO BUY IN AS *PARTNER*. TO BE PART *OWNER* OF THE PLACE. IT'S PART OF THE *CONCEPT*, YOU KNOW?

LOONY LEO'S RESTAURANT -- IT'S A BETTER HOOK THAN LOONY LEO WORKING *IN* A RESTAURANT, RIGHT?

"LOOKING BACK ON IT, I WONDER IF THEY JUST DIDN'T HAVE ENOUGH MONEY *THEMSELVES*.

"BUT AT THE TIME, I WAS JUST *SCARED*. GOING OUT, FACING THE *PUBLIC* AGAIN --

"-- AND IF IT FAILED, I'D HAVE LOST MY STAKE -- I'D BE OUT ON THE *STREET* AGAIN --

191

"BUT STILL -- BUT *STILL* --

"ANYWAY, IT'S BEEN...*OKAY.*

"I LIVE UPSTAIRS, I WATCH THE *FOOD COSTS*, AND I MAKE SURE THE BARTENDERS POUR A DECENT *DRINK.*

"I COME OUT EVERY NIGHT, AND I PLAY MY PART AS *HOST* -- INTRODUCING THE *PIANO PLAYER* --"

GOOD EVENING, FOLKS, AND *WELCOME* TO LEO'S. THIS *ISN'T* DOOLEY WILSON AT THE PIANO, AND AS YOU'VE PROBABLY *NOTICED* -- -- *I'M* NOT HUMPHREY BOGART.

HA HA HA HA HA HA HA HA

"-- MINGLING WITH THE *CUSTOMERS*, ASKING IF THEIR FOOD'S GOOD, SIGNING *AUTOGRAPHS* --

"THE KIDS *LOVE* IT. AND THE ADULTS -- THEY SEEM TO LIKE THE SHEER *WEIRDNESS* OF IT.

"THEY COME *BACK*, ANYWAY.

"AND AT THE END OF THE *NIGHT* -- AT THE END OF THE NIGHT, EVERYONE'S *GONE* --

"-- SO I GO BACK UPSTAIRS AND I WATCH *OLD MOVIES* AND WAIT TO DO IT AGAIN *TOMORROW*.

"IT *WORKS.* IT FILLS THE *DAYS.*"

AND NOW HERE *YOU* ARE. YOU WANT ME BACK ON *TV.*

YOU WANT ME DOING COMMERCIALS FOR -- WHAT WAS IT, A *GARAGE?*

AND YOU CAN STILL SIT THERE AND *ASK* ME THAT, AFTER ALL I'VE *TOLD* YOU?!

Ah, A CAR DEALERSHIP.

Snapshots

One of the most enjoyable parts of creating a city is filling it with people. Whether they're heroes or villains, fantasy creatures or ordinary people, they've got to be engaging, distinctive, expressive and memorable. And luckily, working with artists of the caliber of Brent and Alex makes it easy to achieve those goals, no matter what I might throw at them. Herewith, some examples...
— KURT BUSIEK

Previous Page: Alex's design for Julius "Uncle Julie" Furst, the William Frawley of the First Family.

Air Ace has only appeared as a statue so far, but even a statue's got to be designed fully — and when you know the guy's going to show up in his own story someday, he's got to be designed carefully as well. For Air Ace, we wanted to combine a classic WWI pilot's look with just enough superhero elements to make him a believable bridge between a pulp hero and a superhero. The emblem on his chest and the wings on his goggles supplied just the right touch.

Thunderhead

It's one thing to say "a gigantic, threatening stormgod made entirely of dark clouds," and another to pull it off. To find the right look for Thunderhead, Alex was inspired by the "Night on Bald Mountain" section of Fantasia, and classical images of the Greek god Zeus. From Alex's original sketch, shown here, Brent developed the final rendition seen in "Welcome to Astro City."

HE SHOULD BE ABOUT THIS LARGE IN COMPARISON TO THE CITY.

It was easy to make Astra believable as a superhero, but we knew the story would hinge on how believable she was as a little girl. Alex did these sketches to capture her youth and innocence in a variety of moods.

The trick with Mister Smartie, Astra's computer-generated schoolteacher, was to make him expressive enough to be a character, while simple enough to look like a hologram. As you can see, Brent's early sketches included hair and detailed eyebrows, but the brows were simplified and the hair eliminated in the finished version, to make him more of an abstraction.

'MR SMARTY'
ACITY #2
VOL II
8-4-96

Kaspian

Kaspian, ruler of the Beast-Men, was a character whose look didn't gel right away. Brent's initial idea *(far left)* was too human-looking, prompting Kurt to do one of his famously-awkward sketches *(center)* in an attempt to make the character more animalistic, and Alex to bring it all together *(below)* in a sly, foxy look that, while inspired by Bill Everett's early version of the Sub-Mariner, had a strongly woodland, feral aspect.

ANOTHER SUGGESTION

ELFLIKE FEATURES SUGGEST A STRETCHING OF THE FACE THAT IS UNNATURAL

NECK BEARS MORE HUMAN RESEMBLANCE OF AN UNNATURAL FACE

RED HAIR

INSPIRED BY DRAWINGS OF LOKI TRANSFORMING INTO A FISH

GYPSY-STYLE PUFFY SHIRT

WRIST BANDS GYPSY-STYLE JEWELRY

NOT NECESSARILY "UNNATURAL" LONG FINGERNAILS

VERY TALL, LONG LEGS

I ALWAYS SAW HIM WITH WILD WAVY HAIR THE TYPE THAT BILL EVERETT DREW WHEN HE FIRST DESIGNED SUB-MARINER. THE FACE COULD ALSO BE LIKE HIS ORIGINAL

IS THE HAIR STILL RED?

VERY MUCH LIKE MYTHICAL LOKI

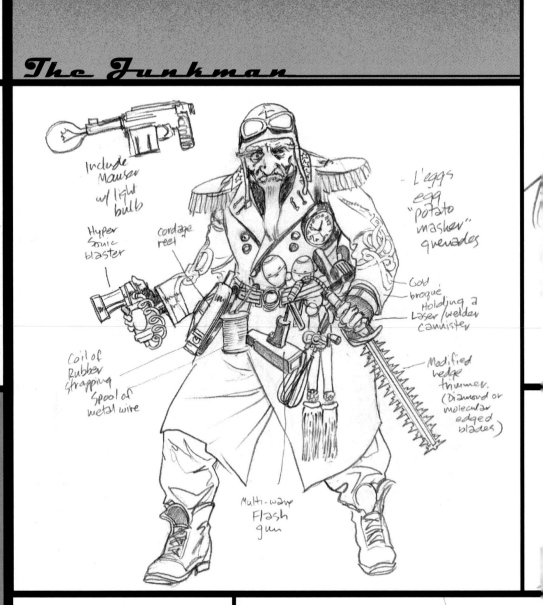

Include
Mauser
w/ light
bulb

Hyper
Sonic
blaster

cordage
reel

L'eggs
egg
"potato
masher"
grenades

Gold
brogue
Holding a
Laser/welder
cannister

Coil of
Rubber
Strapping
Spool of
metal wire

Modified
hedge
trimmer.
(Diamond or
molecular
edged
blades)

Multi-wave
Flash
gun

F or the Junkman, we wanted someone who looked more cranky than dangerous, but who would nevertheless be striking and memorable, and whose gadgetry would be complex and fascinating. The Uncle-Sam beard was Alex's idea (wonder where he got that, hmm?), and the vacuum-cleaner jetpack was Brent's addition. The Mauser with the light bulb was Kurt's contribution, inspired half by a dummy raygun he saw at a convention, and half by Gyro Gearloose's bulb-headed "Helper."

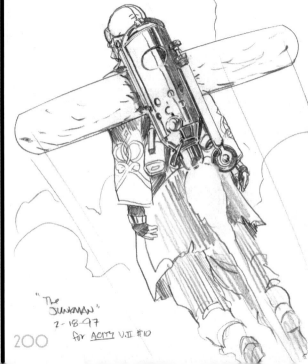

"The
Junkman"
2-18-97
for ACITY V.II #10

Black Rapier

As with Air Ace, we wanted the Black Rapier to look simple and elegant, and a fencer's costume seemed to be the obvious design choice. But the result was too plain, too ordinary-looking, until Alex gave him the combination sash/cape. A minor element, but it was just enough to make him a superhero, rather than simply a fencer with a different-colored outfit.

Jackson & The Box

Jack-In-The-Box's alternate-future sons, The Box and Jackson, represented different design challenges, since unlike most of Astro City's denizens, we didn't want them to look classic or elegant. Instead, we wanted to evoke modern grotesqueries like Cable, Venom and Lobo — but still with a strong family resemblance to their progenitor. Kurt decided that one of them would be an organic monster, and the other a techno-logical one — and Alex took that to heart, delivering a Jackson that featured Jack-In-The-Box's costume elements merged with his own flesh and distorting the human shape beneath, and a Box who'd been mutilated, his body augmented with clunky, functional-but-ugly additions. Justice Jacky was an inspired addition by Alex.

THE "ORGANIC" SON IS A VENOM/SABERTOOTH/WOLVERINE TYPE

RED HAIR IN BOZO - WOLVERINE STYLE. MASK SHOWS ALL EXPRESSION LINE AND VEINS!

WHITE FACE & NECK

YELLOW EYES AND TEETH

TEETH GO ALL THE WAY BACK UP THE CUT OF MASK... IF IT IS A MASK.

BLACK SKIN EXPOSED ON CHEST AND LEGS

ALL MUSCLES WELL DEFINED WITH THE COSTUME DETAILS

BIONIC IMPLANTS

JACK IN THE BOX ARM REPLACEMENT

RED & GREEN STRIPED SHORTS

BIONIC EYE

NO COSTUME WRINKLES

A BLACK MAN WITH WHITE MAKEUP JUST OVER HIS HEAD

RED LIPS

STILT MAN STYLE REPLACEMENT LEGS

INSTEAD OF A PROSTHETIC HAND THERE IS A MECHANICAL PUPPET WITH KNIVES.

JACK — N' — BOX!

202

Zachary

Zachary Johnson, the face behind the mask of Jack-In-The-Box, was the emotional center of "Serpent's Teeth" and "Father's Day," and as such had to be a good enough "actor" to pull the story off. Here, Brent works with Zack's face to make him lively and expressive, while keeping him clearly Zack.

The first conception of Leo was as a cartoon lion in a tux, but something about it didn't seem right. We knew his story was one of disappointment and disgrace, and this dapper fellow didn't seem like he had the range for it.

Below: Expression studies, looking for a way to give Leo the right "hangdog" look. *Below right:* Figure proportion sketches.

TRYING TO SIMPLIFY LIP AND KEEP LIKENESS

less torso

Bogart eyes

One hand almost always in pocket

smokes in "real" life (in deference to the late Joe Camel)

The key to Leo came in thinking of him as a leonine version of Humphrey Bogart in *Casablanca*. The white tux seemed to bring him into this century, and make him a lion of the people, not an elitist snob. Still, something wasn't clicking...

...until he got an abstraction of Bogart's lidded, weary eyes, and his "reality" level was cranked back far enough to make him look like a cartoon among humans, and not just an anthropomorphized jungle beast.

Left: That's a guy who can be a world-weary cartoon!

Alex's design for the Gentleman, the sartorially-impeccable fellow who's been performing well-mannered feats of derring-do in Astro City for coming up on six decades now. He hasn't had much of a chance at the spotlight yet, but he's got quite a history, and quite a story to tell.

And that's the frustrating thing about filling an entire city with such a host of characters. They all have stories — but they've got to wait their turn. So many characters, so few pages...

Cover Gallery

This alternate cover for Vol. 2, No. 1 was designed by John Roshell, incorporating an illustration by Curt Swan and Murphy Anderson

THE JUNK MAN

CYBORG WEARS
OLD '20's STYLE
SWIM TRUNKS
RED & GREEN STRIPED

Father's Day

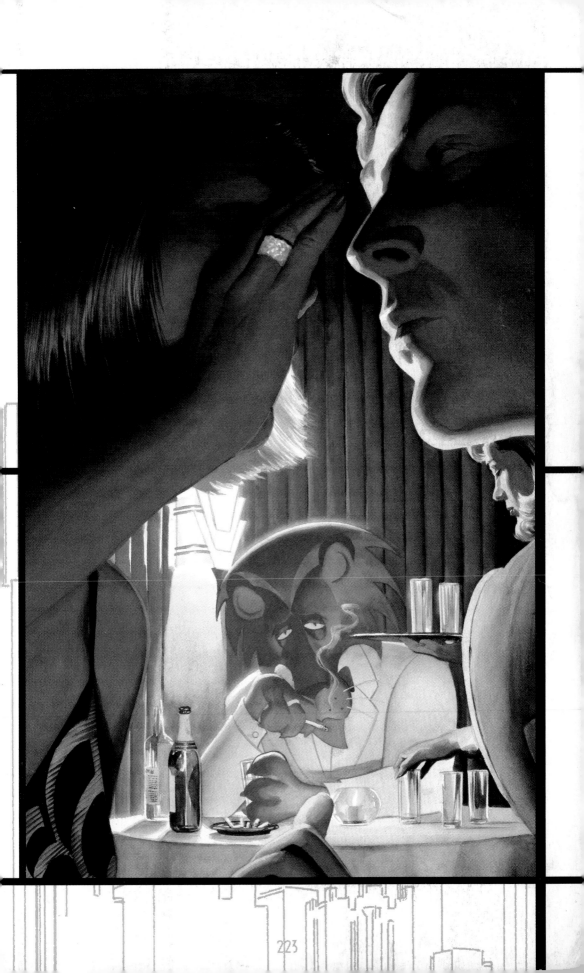

Acknowledgments

My thanks, as always, to the usual subjects for their encouragement and support, from my family bugging me for my next issue to my friends offering up advice, ideas or just an ear when it was needed. And this time around, specific thanks to Lawrence and Julie Evans for chemistry advice, and to Barbara Kesel's father, Jim Randall, for the 414B Hotshot. Also, special thanks to Jonathan Peterson, Astro City's editor for all of the stories included in this volume and the previous one — we may have given you ulcers and made you tear out your hair, Jonathan, but it was a pleasure working with you.

— Kurt Busiek

Thanks go to the many concentric rings of family around me; to my wife Shirley and son Bryce, for the hours they grant me to draw this book; to my mom Carol, sister Cinda, nephew Cody, my brother Aaron and his new family Carol, Adam, Ben and Robyn for their support; to my eternal brothers Frank, Ken, Gary, Chuck, Ron, and Stan for being a constant source of joy and irritation; to Walter Sauers, a Spellbinder forever; to Archie Goodwin, an uncle to us all; and a heartfelt thank-you to two guys in Oaktown who had the courage to say this book makes a difference.

— Brent Eric Anderson

My thanks to my models Ophelia Clark, Greg Gill, Mike Reidy, Ken Kooi, my pop and all my dolls for posing for the covers. I have a brother and two sisters if anybody cares, but they really didn't do anything to contribute to this so they don't bear mentioning by name.

— Alex Ross